ANGELIS
PUBLICATIONS

Published by Angelis Publications
ISBN: 978-0-9956949-7-2
www.angelispublications.com
Cover Design Angie J Anderson

A Celebration of the Life of

_____

_____

_____

_____

_____

_____

"That we once enjoyed and deeply loved we can never lose, for all that we love deeply becomes part of us."

Helen Keller

Name & Address

Thoughts & Memories

Name & Address

Thoughts & Memories

Name & Address

Thoughts & Memories

Name & Address

Thoughts & Memories

Name & Address

Thoughts & Memories

Name & Address

Thoughts & Memories

Name & Address

Thoughts & Memories

Name & Address

Thoughts & Memories

Name & Address

Thoughts & Memories

Name & Address

Thoughts & Memories

Name & Address

Thoughts & Memories

Name & Address

Thoughts & Memories

Name & Address

Thoughts & Memories

Name & Address

Thoughts & Memories

Name & Address　　　　*Thoughts & Memories*

Name & Address

Thoughts & Memories

Name & Address

Thoughts & Memories

Name & Address

Thoughts & Memories

Name & Address

Thoughts & Memories

Name & Address

Thoughts & Memories

Name & Address

Thoughts & Memories

Name & Address

Thoughts & Memories

Name & Address

Thoughts & Memories

Name & Address

Thoughts & Memories

Name & Address

Thoughts & Memories

Name & Address

Thoughts & Memories

Name & Address

Thoughts & Memories

Name & Address

Thoughts & Memories

Name & Address

Thoughts & Memories

Name & Address

Thoughts & Memories

Name & Address

Thoughts & Memories

Name & Address

Thoughts & Memories

Name & Address

Thoughts & Memories

Name & Address

Thoughts & Memories

Name & Address

Thoughts & Memories

Name & Address

Thoughts & Memories

Name & Address

Thoughts & Memories

Name & Address

Thoughts & Memories

Name & Address

Thoughts & Memories

Name & Address

Thoughts & Memories

Name & Address

Thoughts & Memories

Name & Address

Thoughts & Memories

Name & Address

Thoughts & Memories

Name & Address

Thoughts & Memories

Name & Address

Thoughts & Memories

Name & Address

Thoughts & Memories

Name & Address

Thoughts & Memories

Name & Address

Thoughts & Memories

Name & Address

Thoughts & Memories

Name & Address

Thoughts & Memories

Name & Address

Thoughts & Memories

Name & Address

Thoughts & Memories

Name & Address

Thoughts & Memories

Name & Address

Thoughts & Memories

Name & Address

Thoughts & Memories

Name & Address

Thoughts & Memories

Name & Address

Thoughts & Memories

Name & Address

Thoughts & Memories

Name & Address

Thoughts & Memories

Name & Address

Thoughts & Memories

Name & Address

Thoughts & Memories

Name & Address

Thoughts & Memories

Name & Address

Thoughts & Memories

Name & Address

Thoughts & Memories

Name & Address

Thoughts & Memories

Name & Address

Thoughts & Memories

Name & Address

Thoughts & Memories

Name & Address

Thoughts & Memories

Name & Address

Thoughts & Memories

Name & Address

Thoughts & Memories

Name & Address

Thoughts & Memories

Name & Address

Thoughts & Memories

Name & Address

Thoughts & Memories

Name & Address

Thoughts & Memories

Name & Address

Thoughts & Memories

Name & Address

Thoughts & Memories

Name & Address

Thoughts & Memories

Name & Address

Thoughts & Memories

Name & Address

Thoughts & Memories

Name & Address

Thoughts & Memories

Name & Address

Thoughts & Memories

Name & Address

Thoughts & Memories

Name & Address

Thoughts & Memories

Name & Address

Thoughts & Memories

Name & Address

Thoughts & Memories

Name & Address

Thoughts & Memories

Name & Address

Thoughts & Memories

Name & Address

Thoughts & Memories

Name & Address

Thoughts & Memories

Name & Address

Thoughts & Memories

Name & Address

Thoughts & Memories

Name & Address

Thoughts & Memories

Name & Address

Thoughts & Memories

Name & Address

Thoughts & Memories

CPSIA information can be obtained
at www.ICGtesting.com
Printed in the USA
BVHW012119130222
628920BV00003B/103